C0 BVE 367

Crusoe

Crusoe

poems selected and new

Eli Mandel

Anansi
Toronto

The poems in CRUSOE were selected by Margaret Atwood and Dennis Lee. They were drawn from *Trio* (Contact Press, 1954), *Fuseli Poems* (Contact Press, 1960), *Black and Secret Man* (Ryerson, 1964), *An Idiot Joy* (M.G. Hurtig, 1967), and *Stony Plain* (Press Porcépic, 1973). Evie Mandel first noticed that "Transition Table" could be used as a found poem.

Thanks are due to the Canada Council and the Canada Foundation for various awards and assistance, particularly to the Council for a recent Arts Award which helped provide the time for the work needed to complete this selection.

Copyright © Eli Mandel, 1973.

Cover design: Karen Loconte
Cover photo: Graeme Gibson

House of Anansi Press Ltd.
35 Britain Street
Toronto, Canada

Printed in Canada by The Hunter-Rose Company

ISBN: 0-88784-127-9
Library of Congress Card Number: 73-75842

99
1347
7

This is for **Peggy** and Dennis

in the dark wood, a way

186042

Table of Contents

CRUSOE

Greek men dance alone.
The Hebrew yells at stone.
Others eat glass.
Name your own vice, Englishman.

2

The snail's trace:
doubtful words.

Do not ask how I have come
to an exact madness
or what my keepers name
the frenzy of compliant sense.

The dancer alone in his dance
utters the terrible sound of his limbs.

3

This was written for a foundling,
alien, Greek, Hebrew,
to the memory of my sane parents,
in order not to go mad,
and for my keepers' sake,
that I might learn
singular love

no other is to blame.

MINOTAUR POEMS

I

It has been hours in these rooms,
the opening to which, door or sash,
I have lost. I have gone from room to room
asking the janitors who were sweeping up
the brains that lay on the floors,
the bones shining in wastebaskets,
and once I asked a suit of clothes
that collapsed at my breath, and bundled and
crawled on the floor like a coward.
Finally, after several stories,
in the staired and eyed hall,
I came upon a man with the face of a bull.

II

My father was always out in the garage
building a shining wing, a wing
that curved and flew along the edge of blue air
in that streamed and sunlit room
that smelled of oil and engines
and crankcase grease, and especially
the lemon smell of polish and cedar.
Outside there were sharp rocks, and trees,
cold air where birds fell like rocks
and screams, hawks, kites, and cranes.
The air was filled with a buzzing and flying
and the invisible hum of a bee's wings was honey
in my father's framed and engined mind.
Last Saturday we saw him at the horizon
screaming like a hawk as he fell into the sun.

III

They chose among us in the fall of the year,
by lot, behind fierce masks designed of sign
to ward off the imminent descent of the sun people;
someone talked of a dying god, as if
the young ones among us believed in
that any more, others cautioned us against the voices
we were always supposed to hear and these
were stubborn about the women crying.
I remembered the face of one who brought me here
when they drew my name in the hall,
it was her persuasion in the beginning,
something about fathers.
                                    Like the others before me,
I saw only their breasts that appeared on the walls,
legs moving in unison, the swaying of sweat-stained
bodies and their half closed eyes:
all the talk about signs when I knew
the boys were only waiting for the
women to undress, as they always did,
                                    snickering
and those same fields that make a dawn in vision
where birds begin to live in rocks and screams.
It is hard to feel free of accusation
because of eyes
although there is a difference between revelation
and action bellied into life, between
believing in voices
and knowing the chances that we have to take.

IV

Now I am dressed in a multitude of rooms
like a Chinese box, and slip from covers
into covers   Dawn will not help me nor
the day's exposure I am a prodigious pun
to hide and show myself between these walls
this otherwise where sunlight
dressed in a tweed suit pursues me
or a stranger in the rooms
          and footfalls on the stairs
and eyes   and over all
    the whispering and chattering of the walls
          the pipes and hammered arteries of the place.

Is that a revelation in a field of light
competing with a shadow on the rock?
A bird's shadow seen from here?
Or a cloud between the sky and land
footed and patterned into phrases?

It is hours since I have been in here.
If I had once seen anything
except birds,
rocks, land, and all winter long
                    the ice and snow

V

Within these walls I am to look for light
Or hold an abstract in my hand as firm
As apples or the golden bar the older men
Returned to us. Remember that. That spring
There were those crowds and crowds below the cliffs
This side of town and all along the beach,
Flags out, booths filled with toys, and one,
The better salesman of the lot, a beggar
From the north had miniatures of bars
That went like hotcakes. Fleece for the crowd.
A replica to keep you as it kept our men
This winter past. Then noise, flocks wheeling overhead,
The painted ship, a bauble on the sea, came like a toy
To harbour.
                    And the tall bronzed men descended
Between the cheers and speeches at the harbour mouth,
Talk about campaigns in lands we'd never heard of,
Cheers and lewd remarks and laughter, the look
In other eyes, and counting of the crew
And stooping at the gaps aghast.
That was another death, the shock in surf,
The rock's point of view, the hawk
Momentarily composing before the fall
His target of a landscape from the sky.
The trailing plume before the dark.

Night on the beach
         and smoke
         from new charred campfires.

VI

ORPHEUS

The Welshman by the pit whose Sabbath voice
Would set the week to peace,
Picked over coal and said he knew
The inside of our god, his transformation
Out of tree, the face in black,
Stamped on the walls he picked. This metaphor,
He said, the pit shaped underneath him into black
And pitied words that moved the leaves or sang
Together flocks, or shook the dull and herded animals.

His pity also took between the rocks
Some still alive who saw the black and second
Hand that clawed them, and he mocked in Welsh
Whatever shades fell back, and cursed and sang
Back to their second death those grave ghosts.

Who found his body and who found his head
And who wiped god off his eyes and face?

ESTEVAN SASKATCHEWAN

A small town bears the mark of Cain,
Or the oldest brother with the dead king's wife
In a foul relation as viewed by sons
Lies on the land, squat, producing
Love's queer offspring only,
Which issue drives the young
To feign a summer madness, consort with skulls,
While the farmer's chorus, a Greek harbinger,
Forecasts by frost or rings about the moon
How ill and black the seeds will grow.

This goodly frame, the earth, each of its sons,
With nature as a text, and common theme
The death of fathers, anguished in betrayal
From the first family returns a sacrifice
Of blood's brother, a splintered eyeball
Groined in the fields, scarecrow to crows.
This warns Ophelia to her morning song,
Bawdy as a lyric in a pretty brain gone bad,
While on those fields the stupid harvest lies.

ICE PALACE

Only the blue men
of Saskatchewan
and the blue women
of Quebec

swim these white bone halls
the palace of King Skeleton
and only blue ones could.

Journey through his land alone.
For blue men do not speak
the way you speak, or cry
hail and farewell.

They squeak
like eels on ice

or needles on a gramophone.

PROLOGUE

I think it was burned on. And the smell:
No one would go near it for days after it appeared.
There was hell to pay in the council, everyone
Dredged muck out of the past. The mayor quit.

They tried whitewash. Seen it anyhow, blacker
Than sin on Sunday. Tried burning. Smoke choked
The town for days, the fence was still there.

Bees swarmed, honey of smoke, out of the old
Witch tree and got into the kitchen chimney,
Stung the cook and she quit too.
Slop all over the wall where she threw the pail.
The air was blue with bees and words.

Preacher says,
                Hell fire aint good enough.
Preacher says,
                It burns and it aint burned.
Kind of like drought. The day's coming.
The fine critter bouncing on the hill
Aint the same when she's laid low.
Skinned she's awful.
Like the insides of a calving cow.

And you can't blow the spots off a leopard anyhow.

EPILOGUE

When our mayor was put out to eat grass
And on the street manholes opened like eyes,
Everyone said it had come from below
Because the street was nervous, empty,
And the sewers rumbled for days, the wires
Sang in the high wind and cracks appeared
In the grey cement like folds in an elephant's hide.

Everyone said it had come from below
Because the banks toppled over like great gods
And fire flamed out of the mouth of the stock exchange,
And our bird-like mayor, a hoofed thing,
Galloped away to the green fields in the country.

MAIL ORDER CATALOGUE

(logos of things in the outhouse
paradigm of experience
from beginning: abdominal belts
to end: zippers, lightning

the art of communication
icons of the graffitic world):

bound, stretched, boned women
hung by the harps of their hair
the wire of their thighs

unravished brides   fence
an acre of grass, a seed plot

and what mysterious rites
of harrow, plot, and drill

and hired men walking on the hill
all in a blaze of fire, the wire
strung from their hands like harps
fencing the acres

                  stays, pants,
the attic urn, scored in the grain
a low relief, a lowing heifer,
a bull on the wall.

SOURIS VALLEY

You will ask how I came here. In my 36th year
by libraries and paintings, and the landscape
now northern, a bruised sky, punctured by pines,
and how the university could tolerate me,
what night it was I hung from the rock
and whether my father knew.
                              I met
murder on the way and the face of a Principal,
in the rock I saw the hands of moralists
and the drowned officer who served my warrant
crying, on my rock this first church.

You will understand how much of this is description,
how in the valley mothers would gather, the river
swollen, the mustard milky and sticky, breasted plant,
and how icy sons blossomed like crystal.

DEPARTURE

There was merely a brief note:
"Have seen Edmonton
am leaving at once."
                    I think:
it must have been the buildings
or perhaps the art gallery
or even the university.

But his friends tell me
he had no ambition
his children were slovenly
recently he recovered from a strange disease
he no longer knows what numbers are
nor understands the language spoken here.

DOLL ON THE MANTELPIECE

Here on the mantel where a Dresden doll
Looks into a frozen german hill
All is still, chill, white,
Except the red stain on her lips,
The blood of colour there.

She is poised for a dance above the fire,
A hand out for a partner neither here
Nor anywhere. The fire breathes below
A savage noise of wood and she looks out
Over the white hill, still as a doll,
Chill in her world of ivory.

Why do I think of clowns, of emperors,
Of Nietzsche in his tower and all Berlin
Falling in flames while this silly doll
Stands on a fire, calm beside a frozen hill?

DUCKS IN A POND

1

Hairy and huge, old sun stood
up to his neck in a slough
and ever from his coronal arm
coins to mallards he threw
and mallards in a spume of mire
leaped to the touch of web and fire.

2

One must have a cold, reedy skin
(touching this question of fire)
to tread out a frothy zeal
under the armpits of a hairy wheel
under the arm of the sweating sun
to maunder in a slough of sweat
and skin, of water touched by fire.

3

About the death of ducks in ice
I know nothing, but mallards know
of Franklin underfoot, his men
on Boothia and their frozen dance
in snowy froth that stoned the eye,
the sun a cataract in a blinding day.

4

The zeal of ducks for noise
(touching this question of fire)
is not the music that I hoped to hear
(Isaiah's coal, the final choir)
but poise of mallards in a pool
as in the pupil of an eye where fire
burned on water seems a pose of praise
sufficient for the gabble of my days.

NOTES FROM THE UNDERGROUND

A woman built herself a cave
  and furnished it with torn machines
  and tree-shaped trunks and dictionaries.
Out of the town where she sprang
  to her cave of rusting texts and springs
  rushed fables of indifferent rape
  and children slain indifferently
  and daily blood.

Would you believe how free I have become
  with lusting after her?
       That I have become
  a melodramatist, my friends ashamed?

I have seen by the light of her burning texts
  how the indifferent blood drips
  from the brass mouths of my friends,
  how at the same table I will eat
  and grow fat.

Her breasts are planets in a reedy slough.
Lie down beside that slough awhile
  and taste the bitter reed.

Read in the water how a drowning man
  sings of a free green life.

THERE IS NO ONE HERE EXCEPT US COMEDIANS

1

In what we call dreams I see
a fairground of wheels inside wheels
where I am turned into nobody
nobody's son nobody's daughter

and orphanages
where children
drag toward iron gates yellow dolls
and huge rolling balls
made in the shape of towering fathers

2

I pray nightly for release
I ask of a door shaped like a bat
to fly away with me
I want to be in a wheatfield
stupid as grain yellowing in the sun
I want to be something like a bird,
part reptile, able to stare blankly
for minutes
        at jade trees
        at jewelled grass
        the crystal city

whispering blasphemy
I want to walk over the doors of the city
my bird feet tinkling at keyholes

I want you to know I am innocent
I want you to open the last door
into the field of orphan wheat
the orient grain the green golden corn

TWO PART EXERCISE ON A SINGLE IMAGE

I

I come into the desolation
Of this calm September town
Which slants out of morning
Into the wild disaster of sunlight,
And I see that my street is a tree
Split into a thousand sentences
Any one of which can hang me.
The sun shatters my tree
In a wind of light
Into a torch in the unexplained
Interior, luminous with volcanoes,
Dark fig trees, and the white
Question mark of a polar bear.

II

You think it's easy? A matter of words?
You wonder that I'm a poor speller?
Let me tell you this has nothing to do with
Teaching, or even the love of poetry.
It is an eyesore, a stye,
A social disaster. Look for once
At the real, ridiculous self
Crouched in the unexplained interior.
See it looming in the light of
Exploding volcanoes, dark fig trees,
Like the hunched white question mark of
A polar bear.
                    Oh my friend
I too like company
And have ambitions in business.

SONG

When the echo of the last footstep dies
and on the empty street you turn your empty eyes,
what do you think you will see?
A hangman and a hanging tree.

When there are no more voices
and yet you hear voices singing
in the hot street,
what do you think will be their song?
Glory to the hangman who is never wrong.

When on the hot sands of your burning mind
iron footsteps clang no more
and blind eyes no longer see
and voices end,
what do you think will be your plea?
Hanging isn't good enough for me.

THE GOLD BUG

a poisonous bee burst his pod
in the palm of my hand
                                    his venom
flowed over my hand like honey

now honoured among men
I gesture with my golden hand
and I speak with the language of money

PALINODE

I don't suppose that poems can be made
Of private shame, of shame, or sham
Excesses of the spirit.
                              Modest Locke
Once closed the door to godliness
And in his shaded room saw nothing
Of the wide, bruised sky of spring.
He said, the underbrush is thick,
Until we've hacked a way through it
We cannot know the shape of practical despair.

I say that it was spring,
And it was then as if with prison bars
The ruler sun had strictly lined the air,
As if a kind of Dali plain, empty of bush,
Stretched out, as if the first ants
Of the year crawled on the sky,
And it was then I saw that private men
Were dragging loads of bone and flesh
In sackfuls to the edges of the plain.
I cried to stop it, saying, God, you know,
Inhabits each man's breast. Look at the sky,
The sun is Blake in excess of his glory
Come to clothe the naked twigs, and looked
And saw the drop of blood that hung there
And saw it run and spread and soak the men
And saw it seeping, in the spring, out of those sacks.

THE FIRE PLACE

A furnace is of stone and clay,
A fire burns inside the stone,
Beside the flame Fuseli lay,
The heart within it was his own.

Fuseli, when the witch came in,
Raised the roof above his stone,
On her thighs he painted sin,
On her head a horse's mane.

From her lips a vocal moth
Issued screaming to the smoke,
Augustan ladies in their mirth
Gathered folds about her smock.

In the smoking cup a sea,
By the bed a painted ship,
In the door a massive key,
On the floor an open trap.

Coupled with a horse a man
Leans upon her breast; he sighs;
Flaming curtains issue then
In between the witch's thighs.

PILLAR OF FIRE

A man came to my tent door
in the heat of the day, the tent
stretched and slapped in the wind.
All the guy ropes went taut
and I felt my temples stretch
and throb in the noise and heat.

He talked about blowflies,
plague among the swollen cattle.
He asked about the children.
"You are a great nation.
Will you stay here long?"

That night the fire in the tent
vomited a great smoke.
The tent glowed like a furnace.
I dreamt about Egypt and its flies,
a priest dying of cancer.
I am told to breed more children,
try not to think about politics,
remember the Sabbath and my enemies.

MR MANDEL'S SERMON

I have heard singing and thought how singing maddens
the singers because their mouths are open in a shriek
and the strained muscles of the faces pull down the eyes
in a clown's cry.

        Around the stake where the dying bear
has lolled for several days the singers are open-mouthed
and at the pit where the bear baited the virgin

                where
the court musicians squeezed the rare mouth-sweat
into the petals of their horns like bees dripping
honey on the horns of lilies

        the song was a bridegroom
pacing his claim to the tent of his blue bride.

This cosmic song was sung my murderous friends
by you who raped the bear's girl before you hurled
her in the pit and you in whom the stake is never still.

MAP OF LOVE

I was sure that his children were lousy
and his wife's eczema thickest
around her thighs
                    like a map
of a tyrant's gradual conquest
of Europe
            or a medical diagram
of the advanced tumours of love.

METAMORPHOSIS

Looking at her, my eyes magnified by anger,
I saw her nose collapse to nostrils in her face,
her eyes narrow, her eyelids disappear,
her lips extend into a pointed, yellow beak;
I thanked the transformation of my rage
that gave me vision.
                    Later,
I discovered my eyes were little stones
and on my hand instead of hair were quills,
and in my blood, not hers, the reptile crawled.

Intellectual beauty, how we are shrunken now.

THE OTHER HARMONY: NOT IMITATION

Nothing simple: a particular lie
spreads like ink on a Rorschach card
like clouds upon the moon
                        and she
in the inky arms of the octopus
deep in the bottled sea
                        and dizzily
is my squalid, squat, and masculine
mother.

       I made this (decked out
as a dandy) and I have made other
seas
    and shall again in winter
sail farther than Saskatoon or Calgary.

PICTURES IN AN ASYLUM

The shock is
> do not honour verity
> that lie you told, it is here
> under the sea, under the sea

the shock is
> do not love so many
> love is the stone that tears
> the bladder on the yellow sea

the shock is
> things are what they seem to be
> there is no god
> no love nor verity
> under the sea

and the shock is
> sharp as ice-picks in the brain
> the child is sane
> the child is sane again

CHARLES ISAAC MANDEL

These uplands of the suburban mind,
sunlit, where dwell the lithe ironists,
athletic as greeks, boy-lovers,
mathematical in love as in science.
Formalists. What have I to do with them?
I gather the few relics of my father:
his soiled Tallis, his Tefillin,
the strict black leather of his dark faith.

LANDSCAPE

The tree shaped like a lock against the sky
And the river like a door and like a key

The sorrowing sun looks in, there is a rim
Around the world, ships topple from the rim

Into the sun but topple back and still are here,
There is a rim and the river shuts like a door.

The tree shaped like a coffin or a nail
And the river like a dark misshapen door

And the sun crouched in his terrible lair
Looks in on the falling ships, the unmusical

Falling ships, and the trees lined up the wall
Like mourners at my mother's funeral.

JEWISH CEMETERY IN EDMONTON

If one could move bloodlessly
through the razor air
                    but
the white blood of the snow
drips on the wounded earth.

Trees, apprehensive as vines,
quiver over the slit veins.

Who, with his mouth, will stop
this cold blood or put his root
or seed into this vain wound?

DAY OF ATONEMENT: STANDING

My Lord, how stands it with me now
Who, standing here before you
(who, fierce as you are, are also just),
Cannot bow down. You order this.
Why, therefore, I must break
If bend I will not, yet bend I must.

But I address myself to you thus,
Covered and alert, and will not bare
My self. Then I must bear you,
Heavy as you are.
              This is the time
The bare tree bends in the fierce wind
And stripped, my God, springs to the sky.

OVERHEARD AT THE GAZA MILL

I don't like evasion any more than you do
    but to speak out at this time
    is more dangerous than you might think:
    do you know what they burn on Fridays
    and why, and what they carry back?

Even with an inviolate ethic this happens:
    the market brilliant as blood
    soiled relics on the street
    and the athlete carted, a bundle of bones,
    into the ruined stadium, his owners profiting.

DAVID

all day the gopher-killing boys
        their sling-shot arms
            their gopher-cries

the king insisting
    my poetry must stop

I have written nothing since May

instead
        walk among the boys
gopher-blood on their stretched
hands
        murder will end murder
the saying goes, someone must
do something about the rodents
and poems do not:
                        even the doctors
admit that it's plague
ask me about my arms
                look
at my shadow hanging
    like a slingshot

the world turns like a murderous stone
    my forehead aching with stars

SONGS FROM THE BOOK OF SAMUEL

i

the intellect does not age, the body dies
daily the mind declares its lies
about the soul, about the self
about the body and its ageless cries

now mind grows freer as the body dies
daily the body ages in its lies
about the mind, about the self
about the mind's clear sense of paradise

ii

I forgive the adulterer, I forgive the song
I forgive the straw man in my bed
I forgive the old man his lies about the bed
I forgive my armies for their arms
I forgive the generals for their boots
and the mayors for their homes
and the councillors
                    my mother
for her prophecies, my father
for his mistaken comfort in failure
my teachers for their religion
I forgive the girl's face in the flower
the instrumental poet hung on his strings
the colonies for the times they did not eat
I forgive the food of the armies
and the carpets under the general's feet
I forgive the poet for lying about god
I forgive god for tomorrow
I forgive the arisen prophet
the man who is a weapon
the weapon
death
the song
the singer dying in his song
even myself

COLD PASTORAL

I thought someone said cathedral
      stature of gold
      emperor's bird
and eyes through shining hair.

I thought someone said drowning
      gather of weed
      swirling word
and shining eyes through water.

No one ever said ice
      blood
      wind
or eyes in the cadaver

THIEF HANGING IN BAPTIST HALLS

After a Sculpture by George Wallace

Amid the congratulations of summer,
polite vegetation, deans, a presbyterian sun,
brick minds quaintly shaped in gothic and glass,
here where the poise and thrust of speech
gleams like polished teak
I did not expect to see myself.

But there he hangs
shrugging on his hung lines,
soft as a pulped fruit or bird
in his welded soft suit of steel.

I wish he would not shrug
and smile weakly at me
as if ashamed that he is hanging there,
his dean's suit fallen off, his leg cocked
as if to run
or (too weak, too tired, too undone)
to do what can be done
about his nakedness.

Why should he hang there,
my deanship, my insulting self, all undone?

CARLETON UNIVERSITY: JANUARY 1961

To George Johnston

Imagine a speaking rock: stone-dumb
mountains lean over Ottawa
but even the dumb stone spires
of Parliament Hill aspire to speech.

There is something raucous in Ottawa;
the P.M.'s speech is coarse,
brash the Privy Council's course
between Hull and the unspeakable Laurentians.

I think of a child's yell of pain
when he is speared by malicious tables,
explanation animate, mythical, fabulous,
and then of you, articulate climber,
bruised by stony syntax
on the mountains of Gawain's English.

How many beastly tables have you slain
where Carleton and its new cement
utter a few blue nouns and glassy verbs
between the howling trains and muzzled snow?

ON YONGE STREET

After Raymond Souster

seeing your head weave
      your cheeks twitch
      your shoulders jump
I wonder who hit you
      who do you hate

and who will you take on next
      at forty, the punch
      hard as before, reflexes
      quick, your eyes clear

don't you know they will get you
      in the ring or in some alley
      that they will break your mouth
that even the best go blind
      hear unevident birds

or do you care, dreaming of brutes
      buckled and crushed
      the great roar
and the white centre blind with light?

THE COMEDIANS

You might have expected music
But they move so slowly they make no sound.
Like swimmers they put their large hands
Up before their huge red mouths
As if to shove mountains of water
Inches over so they can breathe.

And yet you think you hear gasps,
Snuffling, muffled yelps, occasional
Screams when one wallops the other
Or with a paddle shuffles on his enormous feet
Toward his kneeling unsuspecting friend.

Sometimes in their drowning motions
They remove their arms and heads
And walk in their bodies like barrels.

No longer do I care for those critics
Who plead with me that Whitman is God.
As for that other poet, he was lying too.
Warmed by outlandish currents
I have begun to build an aquarium
Tolerant only for tropical fish
Who move like swimmers without sound
And nuzzle one another with their golden mouths.

SECRET FLOWER

Sometimes you are a house
sometimes you unfold
ages and ages old
    you are sometimes
    a house with four rooms
    and four kings
    and four queens
secret flower
of my own design.

Deeper and more secret
darker and older
you unfold.

I have watched lovers
drop from your petals
into the room of kings
before the table of judges.

How can this be? It is Sunday.
My children are making paper men
no one has been poisoned
no one has been hung
there is even laughter in the room.

Darker and still more secret
older and unfolded
beyond my designing heart
beyond even my crying out
through your four rooms
past the hanging tree
beyond the swaying lovers
beyond the judges

who is that lying on the green carpet?
who is being carried on the stone tablet?
why do these gesture and posture before me?

I kneel before the four-armed god
gather up the shredded paper heads
and turn toward the suddenly open door.

THE DAMP PILGRIM

Was it the mouth?
The air around that castle stank of moat.
Westward a few pilgrims dragged along
Up to the steepled hill now steeped in sun
The growing shadows of their pointed hoods.
And damp inside, damp hung in mist,
Damp hung in ropes of froth along the walls.
I say the brilliant castle stank of moat.

It was in Holland or in Hungary.
The King collected all his furs, and still
He shivered, shook, and cursed the damp.
The Queen wept for her gems.
The pilgrims moved toward the steepled peak.

Clang! went the jester in the court.
He shook his mitred locks and rang
As hollow as a bell hung in a well.
Clang answered from the chains that hung below.

I would leave the court, leave hall, leave
Hollow echoing and damp and find some room
Gone yellow, dry, and dusty with old time
As parched and faded as the pages of my book.

HIPPOLYTUS

Lately I have been dreaming of horses

I have known mothers larger than boxcars
carrying the freight of years and wars
toward some stockyard of their minds
where they can count the slaughtered time

I too know something of punishment
there have been drownings even here
beside the dry reeds of the lakeless fields
hands have been held out to me
I dare not touch beside that unseen water
and once a beaten animal stumbled by
looking like someone's brother

easier then to praise
the strong in one another's arms
testing the machinery of love
the freight that moves the world's
horizons
   everyone knows the rules
what to ignore, when and how to whip
the beaten and to bruise the animals

at the edge of these dark waters
hearing the drums of the world movers
again begins the sound of hoofs
I see the wet heaving horses of a last rain

HOUSE OF CANDY

Larches charred still leaning in the swamp,
I stumble here. What do I know of muskeg?
Woodsmen I have met in stories saved young girls.
It was the smoking hearts of casual rodents
They threw before the queen, her clouded eyes.

If I go forward to the blackened tower,
What must I learn about this offering?
How in my bloodless hands will I take blood
Or how appease the queen, her unencumbered arms?

Hunters darkened stare through sullen smoke
As if to see my shape where larches stand
Or find me in the smouldering stump of pine
Or like some candied house, a crystal rock,
Or marvellous and abstract in a cave,
All bearded whisper and prophetic eye.

They do not know how at the story's end,
Duller than prose, I turned toward the south,
Sought out the urgent maiden, warned her of the queen,
Then drove my knife into her heart to save a passing rat.

A CAGE OF OATS

To James Reaney and Jay Macpherson

How many prisons do I count?
Here is the wall I first ran from
and here there is a second wall,
the wall I ran against to flee
the first, and here there is a cage.

Inside the cage there is a second cage.
Inside the second cage there is a third.

Inside the third
there is a bird.

A Quaker holds a box of oats
on which a Quaker holds a box.
A mirror mirrors oats
for oats are mirrors of their crops
which farmer-quaker-man will thresh
and eat to put the seeds inside
the Quaker man who holds a box.

There may be stars inside of stones
(or other stones): inside of stars
there may be burning seeds.

What boxed bird so great
it can eat
stone, man, star and seed?

CASSANDRA

This has nothing to do with brothels.

Sometimes it seems my daughter or my wife
or my neighbour's wife, bright-eyed,
imitates an image out of sleep. They walk
as if I had dwindled, looking past me
toward unreasonable parliaments
crouching beside senatorial hills.

I have been practising this poetry in secret.
Also I have made advances toward pregnant women.
But there have been no unusual shadows,
all the swimming pools remain clear of blood,
and by the gates the watcher has not raised his arms.

TO MY CHILDREN

A rose grew in my head
My father lay dead
My mother fell among stones
Two flowers grew in my loins

I sing to my blossoming wife
My father is dead
My mother abandoned her life
Why should I lay down my head

Stony and brittle my days
My children sing psalms
The rabbis are ancient and wise
Blessed be my flowering names

NUDE

I apologize to my children
for unplayed games, the Arthurs
I wasn't in the child's nighthood
poetry is a demanding art

sometimes I think I am a city
there is a steel furnace in my heart
trains rush up and down my arms
toward terminals where lovers meet
on the tips of my fingers
my head is a builder's project
full of unsold homes
                        around my thighs
a garden of Boschian animals
carrying bedpans
                somewhere
(inside) loinward? Pancreatic?
Glandular as in brain or neck?
Anywhere there inside
watery and dismal
                        a tremulous
fish and something utterly nude.

THE MEANING OF THE I CHING

                    i

unopened
            book of old men
            orange-blossom book
                            before me
you were
            how could you contain me?

do you not see I am the mouths
of telegraphs and cemeteries?
my mother groaned like the whole
of Western Union to deliver
my message
                and yelling birthdays
that unrolled from my lungs
like ticker-tape for presidents
about to be murdered
                        I sped
on a line that flew
to the vanishing point of the west

before I was
                you were
unopened book
                do not craze me
with the odour of orange-blossom

do not sit there
like smiling old men

        how could you contain me?

ii

under my fingers words form themselves
it's crazy to talk of temples in this day
but light brightens on my page
like today moving against the wooden house
all shapes change and yet stay
as if they were marble in autumn
as if in the marbled yellow autumn
each western house becomes a shrine
stiff against the age of days
under my fingers stiffly formed

I will walk in streets that vanish
noting peculiar elms like old women
who will crash under the storm of sun
that breaks elm, woman, man
into a crumble of stump and bark
until the air is once more clear
in the sane emptiness of fall

iii

my body speaks to me
as my arms say: two are one
as my feet say: earth upon earth
as my knees say: bow down, unhinge yourself
as my cells say: we repeat the unrepeatable

the book speaks: arrange yourself in the form
                   that will arrange you

before I was: colours that hurt me
                arranged themselves in me

before I was: horizons that blind me
                arranged themselves in me

before I was: **the dead who speak to me**
                arranged themselves in me

iv

I am the mouths
of smiling old men

there rises from me
the scent of orange-blossoms

I speak in the words
of the ancient dead

arranged
in the raging sun
in the stiffening age of days

and in the temple of my house

THE MILK OF PARADISE

1

Marvel upon marvel the berries of the sun
inflame the tumbling waters of my limbs
I am given to such visions: wide-eyed
luminous men walk through a hairy land
toward a milky glade where goats bleat

2

I put away this last unfinished poem
to think with trouble of a friend
who wrote me and whose words I scorned

STREETLIGHTS

they're not sunflowers
yet they burn on their stems
like the golden eyes of those other plants

and they bend
in such an iron complaint
toward the street's inverted sky

I'd like to think
they know as much of final things
as any living creature who endures the dark.

WOODBINE

When a crooked man meets beauty
You think there'd be shouting in the streets

Believe me, I have gone about with pails on my head
so that my friends would recognize me

I wish there were no allegories
I wish the doctors could do something about my forked tongue

Lord, Lord, pollution everywhere
But I breathe still
                    and breathless, sweet
woodbine, colour of honey, touches my skin
as if my unbelieving eyes made no difference at all

SIGNATURES

In the eyes of lovers and mothers
gardens recently frighten me, grunts
from earth, deep growing things.
I think of Schweitzer dead at last,
his organs mutilated by those roots.
As for the tumult in the streets,
there are knives in water, in taps,
and once I took up from the tracks
beside the water-tower in my town
a huge beet, hairy and huge, that lay
in my hands like an under-water thing.

Thugs rampage. Marines draw down the head,
ancient and tight, her hair in ecstasy,
some Viet-Nam woman who had loved deeply
or who'd wept over her gunman son,
draw down into a pool that head
I've seen in paintings where there was no blood.

The room is alien: threats uttered
where only the print and I engage
our locked dialogue.
                        Out of the blind
years, remotely, as in earth stirred
by slugs or worms, heaves a memory
of beets and roots; things unuttered
and unutterable, echoing out of print,
out of streams, a signature of rage.

GIRL ON A HIGH WIRE

Do you think I'd sit here staring
if I knew how to work a chair-lift
or lacked this odd taste for vertigo?

What if I dare you to jump, saying, ah
my hurt bird, I will catch you—
and if I weren't there (someone calling,
my son pointing at camels or wanting
to pee) when your eyes became horizons?
Or if you fell
into the well of bankers, mid-wives,
my brother-in-law, the Prudential Life
Insurance Company?
                          I see them,
heroine, hefting you, their applause
ringing your head with the clatter of zircons,
mouths blowing little balloons of praise.

The great globe circles.
Soldiers fall into muddy rivers.
Boys walk the tightrope of their prison yard.

I can no longer look at telephone wires,
the vanishing point of your unfinished portrait.

I shall devote myself to entomology,
practise weight-lifting with dinky toys,
but who will keep me from my crooked prayers,
those mad doves that fling haloes around you?

HOUDINI

I suspect he knew that trunks are metaphors,
could distinguish between the finest rhythms
unrolled on rope or singing in a chain
and knew the metrics of the deepest pools

I think of him listening to the words
spoken by manacles, cells, handcuffs,
chests, hampers, roll-top desks, vaults,
especially the deep words spoken by coffins

escape, escape: quaint Harry in his suit
his chains, his desk, attached to all attachments
how he'd sweat in that precise struggle
with those binding words, wrapped around him
like that mannered style, his formal suit

and spoken when? by whom? What thing first said
"there's no way out?"; so that he'd free himself,
leap, squirm, no matter how, to chain himself again,
once more jump out of the deep alive
with all his chains singing around his feet
like the bound crowds who sigh, who sigh.

THE SPEAKING EARTH

grandfathers fall into it
their mighty beards muffled in grass

and admirals, the sea-sounding men

lovers fall into the earth
like rain on wet dark bodies

listen, our lady earth flowers
into the sea-green language
of grass and drowned admirals

listen: in bearded branches
clasped like broken hands
admiring birds
lovers singing of their kiss
before and after all the words

LISTEN, THE SEA

yes what is
I'm learning

by your leave
leaving
     rising
to leave
      return
and turn
     we
deliberate
by the waves
rhythm casual
move
    tidal

as
  traffic

as
  the sea-women

neither are they
certain uncertain
but with us

within
        their song
here and
            hear
it is

MEDITATION ON THE PAPYRUS OF ANI

sparrows discovering my eyes
leave me undisciplined

a trouble to my family

my soul, my indolent soul
why have you not learned the 66 names of god?

THE WAGGONER'S SONG

I've learned
           not to believe
in those hairy monks with their burning trees

           but that story
about the slain daughter
where we wept in one another's arms
that was good
              now I know
something more about agony
                       I know
perfection is a poem I never wrote

one about children
a tree
a curious bird
              well, there are other songs

THE MADNESS OF OUR POLITY

I saw this. On the prairies where I lived
a boy who put a needle in a gopher's eye
knew more of civil law than all my friends.

What other emblem do you need?

POEM

Lately, the Chinese paintings on my wall
utter profanities
            and yet, no Western man
has set his foot upon those hills
or muddied with his hands that silent waterfall.

THE PRESIDENT AND THE CHAIRMAN MEET

when great men greet each other
with tea and wine and ceremony
small ones draw close
to guard themselves

ON THE DEATH OF HO CHI MINH

toward the end
he became frail as rice paper
his beard whispering thin ideograms

how unlike the great carved storm
that was Marx's face
               how unlike
the darkness and fury
in Beethoven's head
             scarcely
anything to be consumed

bombs destroy   destroy
but cannot touch his body now
or burn his poems

IN THE FIFTY-SEVENTH CENTURY
OF OUR LORD

semitic and secret I plan new evasions,
survival, the tribal rite
                        to be
horribly chummy with god
as if he cared
                in particular
about my politics
my plans for adultery
my marvellous scheme to blame it
on my neighbour's blameless wife

FROM THE NORTH SASKATCHEWAN

when on the high bluff discovering
the river cuts below
                send messages
we have spoken to those on the boats

I am obsessed by the berries they eat
all night odour of Saskatoon
and an unidentifiable odour
something baking
               the sun
never reaches the lower bank

I cannot read the tree markings

today the sky is torn by wind:
a field after a long battle
strewn with corpses of cloud

give blessings to my children
speak for us to those who sent us here
say we did all that could be done
we have not learned
what lies north of the river
or past those hills that look like beasts

LETTER TO BE OPENED LATER

Tell them I did not vote Liberal
though I have taken bribes.
I want them to know that secretly
I admired the old red flag.

If they ask about our gods
explain I did pray to the angels
by all their right names:
                              Mr. President
Your Worship, Dear Sir, Your Honour.

Listen:

I've told my analyst everything
except the bit about the girl student.

I don't know why the inspector threatens me
with letters rimmed in red.

NEITHER HERE NOR THERE

somewhere, I'm told, in fields darker than sleep
browse dreaming beasts with unhurt eyes
while walnut-coloured men in wind-swept voices
revolve their prayers as if they were wheels or stars

it isn't that way: one by one my poems fall apart
like a cooked onion
                    in the next house
a window opens once
                    you wouldn't believe
what my blonde neighbour said
                                anyhow
next year the carnival will be bigger
they say they've got a real live junkie in a rage

THE ANARCHIST-POETS

Step carefully through this rubble of words.
Can you really say which wrecks were once poems,
which weapons?
                    who once ran havoc
through these cities of language
scattering flowers of darkness,
black bursts of unmeaning?
                    what guerrillas
frantic for peace, love, home, nation,
government, even for death itself?

THE APOLOGY

I take back my apology:
                    the table the hassock were not moved
                    the radio opens its great ears
                    to assassinations, weathers, sinkings
                    but its four white eyes do not blink
                    its clock goes round
                    I want to connect with the radio
                    I want to put its plugs in my ears
                    and hear my throat announce that even
                    the Leafs are winning
                    I want the table to appreciate my
                    delight in its leaves: I will stand on
                    four legs and try hard to be wooden and
                    brown with folding leaves
                    I will fold and unfold my leaves
                            like a wooden butterfly
                    and birthday cards can be put on me
                    I will support birthday cards and letters
                    demanding rooms in hotels/   and
                                            typewriters
                    connecting tables and stars
I will love the light olive of the Olivetti
if necessary I will drink olive oil
I have no objection to becoming an olive myself
even in a martini
even a bugged martini

but though before my spread hands
though before the blessings and welcomes
in the fake Hebrew gestures I make to
the world
though my agony neither burns nor moves
tables and radios/   and my love does
                              nothing
          oh nothing to change them
I'm not going to apologize
I take back all the sorry clowns I tried to give you
(I will give them to you again, being a dream of Chaplin and
the short-haired girls who flicker in his hunch-backed gaze)
because you are not the table or radio
because you are not the idea of an olive or an olive
or an olive's idea of itself
because I can be tables but not you
and all the words fall hopelessly at your feet
like the bad idea of a plastic bouquet in hot weather
or the new kinds of toys which never quite fit in their parts
or that Zeppelin *Mad* magazine once tried to make me make
and it couldn't not only not fly it couldn't be put together
to fly though I managed the first three parts of a Voop
which is a great mouth and one foot and things hanging around
the mouth and foot
                    let me work hard at becoming tables or radio
                    I will be precise and they will continue
                    as if I weren't there at all

PSALM 24

What did you expect?
You, who drove me to mad alphabets
and taught me all the wrong words.

Isn't it enough that I've failed?

It's your scripture. You read it.

HEBRAISM

The law is the law and is
terribly Hebrew which is as you
know mostly poems about cooking
and meat to be cured in water and
salt and children to be counted
for pages of generation amid clean
and also unclean women

PICTURES IN AN INSTITUTION

1

Notice: all mirrors will be covered
the mailman is forbidden to speak
professors are confined to their offices
faculties no longer exist.

2

I speak of what I know,
how uncle Asher, spittle on his lips,
first typed with harvest hands the fox
across a fence and showing all good men
come to their country's aid rushed off to Israel
there to brutalize his wife and son

how step-grandfather Barak wiped
sour curds out of his curly beard
before he roared the Sabbath in my ears
what Sara, long his widow, dreamed
the night she cried: God, let him die at last,
thinking perhaps of Josef who had lost
jewels in Russia where the Cossack rode
but coughed his stomach out in Winnipeg

Your boredom does not matter. I take,
brutal to my thoughts, these lives, defy
your taste in metaphor; the wind-break
on the farm that Barak plowed to dust
makes images would ruin public poetry.

The rites of love I knew:
how father cheated brother, uncle, son,
and bankrupt-grocer, that we might eat
wrote doggerel verse, later took his wife,
my mother, in the English way beside my bed.
Why would he put his Jewishness aside?
Because there was no bread?
                                    Or out of spite
that doctors sliced his double rupture,
fingered spleen, and healed his bowel's ache?

Lovers lie down in glades, are glad.
These, now in graves, their headstones sunk,
knew nothing of such marvels, only God, his ways,
owning no texts of Greek or anthropology.

3

Notice: the library is closed to all who read
any student carrying a gun
registers first, exempt from fines,
is given thirteen books per month,
one course in science, one in math,
two options
                campus police
will see to co-eds' underwear

4

These names I rehearse:
                Eva, Isaac,
Charley, Yetta, Max
          now dead
or dying or beyond my lies

till I reeling with messages
and sick to hold again their bitter lives
put them, with shame, into my poetry.

5

Notice: there will be no further communication
                 lectures are cancelled
                 all students are expelled
                 the reading of poetry is declared a public
                                                        crime

NEWS ITEM

man throws himself onto
Ottawa's eternal flame

suffers

superficial burns

(Toronto Star, Oct. 23, 1970)

FIRST POLITICAL SPEECH

first, in the first place, to begin with, secondly,
in the second place, lastly

again, also, in the next place, once more, moreover,
furthermore, likewise, besides, similarly, for example,
for instance, another

then, nevertheless, still, however, at the same time,
yet, in spite of that, on the other hand, on the contrary

certainly, surely, doubtless, indeed, perhaps, possibly,
probably, anyway, in all probability, in all likelihood,
at all events, in any case

therefore, consequently, accordingly, thus, as a result,
in consequence of this, as might be expected

the foregoing, the preceding, as previously mentioned

as already stated

Transition Table
from *Learning to Write* by Ernest
H. Winter (Second Revised Edition)
Macmillan (Toronto, 1961), p.156.

MANNER OF SUICIDE

hanging themselves
taking poison in the top of high trees
throwing themselves on swiftly revolving circular saws
exploding dynamite in their mouths
thrusting red hot pokers down their throats
hugging red hot stoves
freezing to death on piles of ice
in refrigerator cars
lacerating their throats on barbed wire fences
drowning themselves head downwards in barrels
suffocating themselves head downwards in chimneys
diving into white-hot coke ovens
throwing themselves into craters of volcanoes
shooting themselves with ingenious combinations of
a rifle and a sewing machine
strangling themselves with their hair
swallowing poisonous spiders
piercing their hearts with corkscrews and
darning needles
cutting their throats with handsaws and sheepshears
hanging themselves with grape vines
swallowing strips of underclothing and buckles
of suspenders
forcing teams of horses to tear their heads off
drowning themselves in vats of soft soap
plunging into retorts of molten glass
jumping into slaughter-house tanks of blood
decapitation with homemade guillotines
self-crucifixion

Man Against Himself, Karl
Menninger, *passim.*

95

NARRATIVE POEM

the point is
the story
       that
one no one
         told

and yet
       cattle
on lean flanked
land leaning
toward plain

and yet
        shacks
coal fire
despair
       the
barbed wire
wolf willow
river ice

but never
a third act
plotting

end or
even

beginning

land
and long
land
        and
land

PRAISE

even the smallest room
defines
      how we might be
without enclosing space

I praise
      private
secret touching

ESTEVAN, 1934

remembering the family we
called breeds   the Roques
their house smelling of urine
my mother's prayers before
the dried fish she cursed
them for their dirtiness their
women I remember too
                              how
seldom they spoke and
they touched one another

even when the sun killed
cattle and rabbis
                    even
in the poisoned slow air
like hunters
             like lizards
they touched   stone
they touched
                    earth

EDMONTON, 1967

as if by Colville
I mean "hard edge"
stucco   white wall
gravel &
      legs
in one direction shadows
leaning & midget
above the pavement narrows
rapid as the river
              everything
disappears
      neatness: axiomatic
      houses   here
now gone
      "You are impatient
with poetry" my friend writes
from Iceland

OIL REFINERIES: EDMONTON

squat
　　(are)
and there
　　　　fraction-
ary silver re-
flections　flat
distillation
(silver) in
flat
eye
　　pulled side-
ways a slit in
the mind (&) all

a line　against　some
poem
　　　not　there

AT WABAMUN THE CALGARY POWER STATION

leans white in the moon
light puts white slabs up
light shanty whiteness leans

as if it owned the land

daytime horses crop grass
unknowing transformers hum

transformers   at the word
it takes on fiery hair
blazing it transmits
messages furious and hairy
it sends and receives from stars
ancient planets   people
who speak like horses new words

then sparks perform dead
parabolas and loops die
fireplace quietens it is
morning it is light only
the power the power hums

and the lake grows green
again in sunlight
                    it is
morning algae and weeds
thicken
          the green lake
wobbles
          we look at
each other   alien forms

FROM "WABAMUN"

1

lake
   holds
      sun   moon   stars

     trees
       hold

stars   moon   sun

2

only
    waves   motion
    sun   dancing

no sun

only
      light
hurting
in its
    endless
dance

3

on water
many suns
          here there
fires   then
silent comedians
perch jumping

gulls

4

each day I
step
    farther
into dark water

once I will
know
      no longer
whether
      that one
floating
     is myself
or the light
      one
standing
     on the red
pier

5

to have come to this

simplicity

      to know

only

   the absolute

calm
    lake

    before

    night

Anansi Poetry

The Circle Game, *Margaret Atwood*
Power Politics, *Margaret Atwood*
Nobody Owns Th Earth, *bill bissett*
The Gangs of Kosmos, *George Bowering*
Body, *Robert Flanagan*
Incisions, *Robert Flanagan*
Airplane Dreams, *Allan Ginsberg*
The Army Does Not Go Away, *David Knight*
Civil Elegies And Other Poems, *Dennis Lee*
Soundings, *eds. Ludwig and Wainwright*
The Collected Works of Billy
   the Kid, *Michael Ondaatje*
Mindscapes, *ed. Ann Wall*
The Dream Animal, *Charles Wright*
Year of the Quiet Sun, *Ian Young*
I Am Watching, *Shirley Gibson*